BRAINERD INTERNATIONAL RACEWAY

The Can-Am Series at Brainerd International Raceway featured some of the fastest cars driven by some of the country's best drivers. The three-mile layout, with a straightaway nearly one mile long, especially favored the Can-Am cars, which in the early 1970s were unhindered by later rules packages. (Brainerd International Raceway.)

FRONT COVER: Racers warm up for the 1975 Uncola Nationals. One of the most famous racers at BIR, Paul Newman, drove No. 75, a Datsun 510. (Jerry Winker.)

BACK COVER: No racetrack should ever sit idle, but during the long, cold Minnesota winters, it is difficult to run road races. The solution? At BIR, they just race different kinds of machines. (Brainerd International Raceway.)

COVER BACKGROUND: Built on 800 acres of swamp and forest outside of Brainerd, Minnesota, Donnybrook Speedway was inaugurated in 1967. New owners changed the name to Brainerd International Raceway in 1973. (Brainerd International Raceway.)

BRAINERD
INTERNATIONAL
RACEWAY

John Fitzgerald

ARCADIA
PUBLISHING

Published by Arcadia Publishing
Charleston, South Carolina

Library of Congress Control Number: 2013945001

For all general information, please contact Arcadia Publishing:
Telephone 843-853-2070
Fax 843-853-0044
E-mail sales@arcadiapublishing.com
For customer service and orders:
Toll-Free 1-888-313-2665

Visit us on the Internet at www.arcadiapublishing.com

To Michael, Katharine, Anna, and Ilene:
In a life full of mistakes and missteps, you continually give me reason
for hope and happiness.

CONTENTS

ACKNOWLEDGMENTS

Special thanks to Jerry Winker for his invaluable help and to Jed Copham and Geoff Gorvin at BIR.

Frequently used names for courtesies are represented as acronyms:
Brainerd International Raceway (BIR)
Jerry Winker (JW)

The following is a key to abbreviations used throughout the book:
Central Roadracing Association (CRA)
American Motors Corporation (AMC)
International Series of Champions (ISOC)
National Association for Stock Car Auto Racing (NASCAR)
National Hot Rod Association (NHRA)
National Speed Association (NSA)
Sports Car Club of America (SCCA)
United States Auto Club (USAC)

FOREWORD

My wife, Kristi, and I are huge racing fans. It's as simple as that. We love to watch racing, we love to drive race cars, we love everything about racing.

In 2005–2006, we had hoped to build a country club–style racetrack north of the Twin Cities, where people who owned high-performance sports cars could bring them to the track and drive them like they were intended to be driven—fast! About that time, Brainerd International Raceway became available for sale, giving us the opportunity to buy an established track instead of building one from scratch.

We bought BIR and then went to work reviving the road course to create a multi-use motorsports facility. It turned out to be a great decision.

We were familiar with the Lucas Oil NHRA Nationals, which makes a stop at BIR every August, and the track's great amateur drag-racing program, but we also quickly learned how much potential BIR had for being a great road-race track, offering a wide variety of high-level national racing.

So many things make BIR stand out from other racetracks around the country, starting with its location in a small tourism area. It is unique in that the original track has a straightaway 500 feet shy of a mile with a sweeping Turn 1, making them the longest straightaway and fastest turn of any active road course in North America. There is the world-class drag strip, where Tony Schumacher made the fastest run in drag-racing history in 2005 at 337.58 miles per hour. With the addition of the Competition Road Course, the track it is now a multi-use facility.

But, what I really like most about BIR is the rich racing history, with some of the biggest names in racing having competed here. During BIR's second season, in 1969, the United States Auto Club brought its Championship Car Series to Brainerd, along with legendary drivers Al Unser, Bobby Unser, AJ Foyt, Mario Andretti, Gordon Johncock, and Dan Gurney. The Can-Am Challenge Cup was then held here in 1970 with more international racers, followed by Formula 5000, the Trans Am Series with Paul Newman, drag racing, and the list goes on.

Those were drivers who my family talked about around the dinner table when I was growing up. It is still crazy to think that these guys were racing here 40 years ago, at the height of their careers.

Our goal is to continue improving the track to create new memories and carve out a new legacy with racing in Brainerd. Come visit us sometime and find out for yourself what makes BIR so special.

—Jed Copham

Brainerd International Raceway owner Jed Copham is no stranger to racing, and he is willing to put his money where his mouth is. He finished fifth overall in his first Trans Am Series race in 2013, driving a Chevy Corvette for Derhaag Motorsports. (JW.)

INTRODUCTION

To understand Brainerd International Raceway, you have to understand northern Minnesota. To understand northern Minnesota, you have to understand cold—because it gets really cold in northern Minnesota.

Three things happen to people who live in a land where the temperature drops below freezing in November and water does not start to melt until April. First, they become creative with how they spend their time during the winter: ice fishing, snowmobile racing, cross-country skiing, and so on. Second, they squeeze every little bit of enjoyment they can out of the months when the weather is pleasant: hiking, camping, and fishing, as well as weekends watching races at the track.

The third effect weather has on people in northern Minnesota is an understanding of the cycle of change, that when it is nice outside, pretty soon it will be cold, miserable, and wet. They also know that when it is freezing outside and there are only five hours between sunrise and sunset, good days full of warmth, fun, friends, and fuel are ahead.

It is that cycle of boom and bust, of harsh winter followed by pleasant summer, that defines northern Minnesota and its people. And it defines its racetrack as well.

Brainerd International Raceway was built in 1967 and inaugurated in 1968 as Donnybrooke Speedway. It was developed by a group of men who loved racing and wanted a track to scratch that itch.

They built a straightaway that is nearly one mile long, followed by a gentle Turn 1 that can be taken almost at speed. Turn 2 is only slightly less gentle before the racer heads into the flat curves that define the second half of the course.

It was that long straightaway and that gentle Turn 1 that defined Donnybrooke. Racers put their right foot through the floor and barely backed off as they hit the turn, commonly reaching speeds at or over 200 miles per hour.

Donnybrooke was an instant success, with rowdy crowds that filled the large infield and the surrounding towns, much to the consternation of local law enforcement. It drew some of the best racing teams and drivers in the country, and they all praised the new track with its fast times.

But, the boom could not last. Eventually, the track ran into financial trouble and closed in 1972. A new ownership team bought the track in 1973, when it was reborn as Brainerd International Raceway. They were a race-minded group who ran the track well, providing an excellent experience for both fans and racers. All things do change though. By the late 1980s, many of its signature road races had left, and BIR's days of attracting talent on the level of Danny Ongais, AJ Foyt, Rick Mears, Jimmy Spencer, Parnelli Jones, Sterling Moss, Mark Donohue, and Peter Gregg were over. The track's 5,000-foot straightaway is a natural drag strip, which allowed BIR to emphasize drag racing while offering pro racing to operate continuously since 1973.

In 1991, a tornado struck the grounds during the Champion Auto Stores Show and Go, destroying an entire section of the facility.

In 1994, BIR was sold to Michigan businessman Donald Williamson, also known by the honorary title of "the Colonel." Soon, BIR became CBIR, for the Colonel's Brainerd International Raceway. Income in the 1990s and 2000s relied on funding superbike races and using the long straightaway as a drag strip.

The track was sold again in 2006 to Jed and Kristi Copham, who are passionate about racing and who have devoted their time, effort, and resources to revive BIR.

Recognizing the financial benefit of being able to run both drag races and road races every weekend throughout the summer, they built a 2.5-mile road course that uses the back half of the track but does not affect the straightaway. They also purchased a driving school for people who want to experience track racing in either their own vehicles or in track-owned race cars.

BIR is attracting road races again and is in the process of becoming FIA Level 2 certified to host every level of road racing, with the exception of Formula One. In addition to NHRA-sponsored drag races and CRA-sponsored motorcycle races, BIR hosts national-level SCCA Pro Racing events like the Trans Am Series and the Pirelli World Challenge, as well as a variety of regional races. BIR recently hosted the NASCAR K&N Pro Series in 2012 and 2013.

Spring always follows winter. Brainerd International Raceway can survive any bust because a boom is always just around the corner.

The Pinnacle Racing Team of Gregg Rodgers (Chevy Camaro, No. 33) and Scott Ferguson (Pontiac GTO, No. 67) blast out of Turn 12 and into Turn 13 during practice for the 2013 Trans Am Series race. (JW.)

1

THE FASTEST TRACK
IN NORTH AMERICA

A pilot for Northwest Orient Airlines, George Montgomery owned a 427 Cobra but had no place to race it. Over the course of several years in the mid-1960s, he bought 800 acres near Brainerd, Minnesota. One night, he invited former SCCA Land O' Lakes Region founder Bill Peters Sr. to his house, where they surveyed the property's elevation and drainage and, on butcher paper, sketched out the track Montgomery would name Donnybrooke Speedway. (BIR.)

The 3.1-mile track Montgomery created has a straightaway just short of one mile and a sweeping Turn 1 that can be taken almost at speed. (BIR.)

The track, which opened in 1968, was named Donnybrooke Speedway in memory of Donny Skogmo (above) and Brooke Kinnard (below), two local SCCA road racers who died in separate accidents. (BIR.)

This is the first advertising card for Donnybrooke's inaugural season. Created by hand, it promotes not only great racing but also fun in "Paul Bunyan Country." (BIR.)

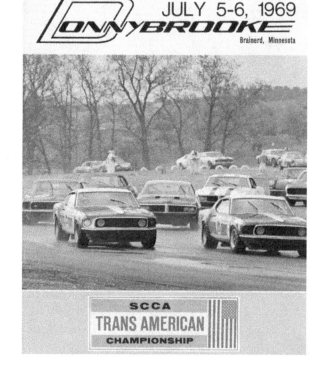

Despite the lack of any concrete safety barriers, grandstands, food vendors, or even restrooms, Donnybrooke Speedway became a must-see attraction in the Brainerd area in the late 1960s. (BIR.)

The tall trees and level elevation gave Donnybrooke a unique feel found nowhere else among American tracks. Tony Ave runs in front with his Corvette, coming into Turn 4 on the first lap of the 2011 Trans Am Series race. (JW.)

Donnybrooke attracted many top drivers from across the country. Mark Donohue (above) won the 1971 Brainerd Trans Am Series race with an AMC Javelin for Roger Penske's team. While most of the cars in that race were Chevrolet Camaros or Ford Mustangs, Peter Revson and Tony Adamowitz drove AMC Javelins, Frank Eggers drove a Pontiac Firebird, and Bob Tullius drove a Pontiac Tempest. Later, Donohue drove a Porsche for Penske, the fastest of which set a Donnybrooke record with an average speed of 125.2 miles per hour, a record that stood for more than 12 years. (BIR.)

THE FASTEST TRACK IN NORTH AMERICA

About one year before he died, Pedro Rodriguez raced in the 1970 Donnybrooke Can-Am Series race, driving a BRM P154. This was the only time he raced at BIR. Denny Hulme won the race in a McLaren M8D, and Rodriguez finished in ninth place. (Tom Winker.)

Swede Savage's Plymouth Barracuda takes on fuel at the 1970 Donnybrooke Trans Am Series race. Again, most of the cars in the race were Chevrolet Camaros, but Donohue had his AMC Javelin, and Parnelli Jones, George Follmer, and Warren Tope drove Ford Mustangs. Sam Posey drove a Dodge Challenger, and Jerry Titus drove a Pontiac Firebird. The Camaro was the smart choice, as 9 of the 11 finishers drove them. The winner was Milt Minter, with Follmer and his Mustang finishing second and Savage and his Barracuda finishing fifth. A member of Dan Gurney's team, Savage would die in a spectacular crash in the 1973 Indy 500. (Tom Winker.)

Oscar Kovaleski drives a McLaren M8B in the 1970 Donnybrooke Can-Am race. Kovaleski also owned the famous Oscar's Auto World in Scranton, Pennsylvania, which sold mail-order model cars and slot cars to gearheads across the country. In 1971, he filled a Chevy van with 76 gallons of fuel and, with Brad Niemcek and Tony Adamowitz, competed in the Cannonball Run from New York City to Redondo Beach, California, finishing second to the team of Dan Gurney and Brock Yates in a Ferrari Daytona. (Tom Winker.)

Quickly developing a reputation as a world-class racing facility, Donnybrooke would routinely draw tens of thousands of fans for races in the late 1960s and early 1970s. (BIR.)

One of the celebrity racers who came to Donnybrooke was comedian Dick Smothers, who in 1968 was just getting his feet wet in the world of racing. He raced the team's B car, while veteran driver Lou Sell piloted the A car. In the 1968 Donnybrooke Grand Prix, Sell's No. 15 Eagle Mk 5 took fourth place. Smothers's Chevron B14 was disqualified after 12 laps with bad bearings. (BIR.)

Lou Sell (left) drove the A car for Dick Smothers (right), who is part of the famous Smothers Brothers variety act. (BIR.)

The 1972 Can-Am race, the Minneapolis Tribune Grand Prix at Donnybrooke, was incredibly loud, featuring machines such as Tom Heyser's Lola T260 (above). Jerry Grant's McLaren M8F (below) did well in the race, which François Cevert won, also in a McLaren M8F. (JW.)

THE FASTEST TRACK IN NORTH AMERICA

After financial troubles had closed the track for a year, stockbroker and racer Jerry Hanson, the winningest driver in SCCA history, bought Donnybrooke Speedway. He and his investors wanted a place name for the track, so they rechristened it Brainerd International Raceway in 1973. (BIR.)

Dick Roe (above) helped turn
around BIR's fortunes. Under
his leadership and that of
Jerry Hanson (left), the track
changed its name to Brainerd
International Raceway and
added drag racing, superbikes,
and even snocross. (BIR.)

Jerry Hansen
Chairman

Dick Roe
President & CEO

David Ames
Vice President & CFO

BRAINERD
INTERNATIONAL
RACEWAY

Mario Andretti
Director

Jack Lundeen
Director

Jerry Hanson made sure his board of directors was a solid group of race-minded individuals. This is a promotional handout of the board from 1973, which, with Hanson and Roe, includes David Ames, Mario Andretti, and Jack Lundeen. (BIR.)

Mario Andretti, shown here with his son Michael, was on the BIR Board of Directors in 1973. He still continues his involvement with racing. (JW.)

The key to a good race team is a good pit crew, and the key to a good track is a good pit facility. Although Donnybrooke Speedway started out lacking in that area, as the track grew in importance, its ability to handle increasingly sophisticated machines and tech inspections grew as well. (BIR.)

THE FASTEST TRACK IN NORTH AMERICA

One of the most famous racers at BIR was Paul Newman. He raced well at the track, winning the 1982 SCCA Trans Am race. Here, his No. 75 Datsun 510 warms up for the Uncola Nationals in 1975. (JW.)

Newman loved racing and wanted to be treated like one of the drivers. He would often sponsor a corn roast where he could break the ice with fans and the other teams as a race car driver, not a Hollywood actor. (BIR.)

OFFICIAL PROGRAM - ONE DOLLAR

The Uncola
Nationals 7up

BRAINERD INTERNATIONAL RACEWAY   JULY 10 & 11. 1976

The Trans Am Series race became the SCCA Uncola Nationals after 7UP agreed to sponsor the event. (BIR.)

Formula Vee cars take Turn 6 during the Jack Pine Sprints in 1980. Although the SCCA's involvement with the track started strong and remained steady for decades, it waned for a period in the 1990s. The SCCA now races regularly at BIR. (JW.)

The Can-Am Series race continued sporadically at Brainerd International Raceway through the 1970s and 1980s. When there was a race, the cars and drivers provided excellent entertainment. (BIR.)

Top drivers, like those on this page, competed in Can-Am races at BIR throughout the years. The winners of the six Can-Am races held at BIR are Denis Hulme (1970), Peter Revson (1971), Francois Cevert (1972), Jacky Ickx (1979), Patrick Tambay (1980), and Michael Roe (1984). (BIR.)

2

THE 3.1-MILE DONNYBROOKE ROAD COURSE

The 3.1-mile Donnybrooke Road Course, although currently only used for club racing, is one of the few racetracks in North America that has not been significantly reconfigured. Turn 1 is a wide, banked, high-speed, 60-degree, right-hand turn that is intended to be taken flat out. Following Turn 1 is a straight, and then Turn 2 is a flat, high-speed, 80-degree, right-hand sweeper that also can be taken flat out. Following Turn 2 is another straight, allowing drivers to regain top speed coming into Turn 3. Here, Derek Thorn's Ford Fusion leads the field out of Turn 3 and into Turn 4 on the first lap of the 2013 Brainerd NASCAR K&N Series West race—the same Turn 3 and 4 that racers in the 1960s would have faced. (JW.)

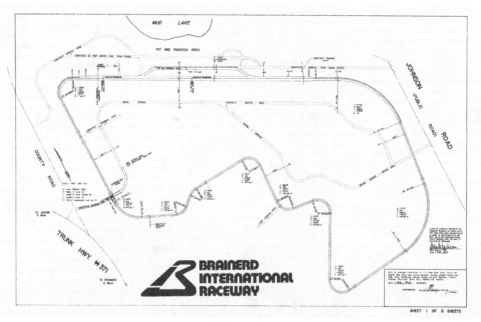

The Donnybrooke Road Course is unique and deserves some explanation. With the help of several experts, the secrets of the track can be revealed. The course is 3.1 miles and has 10 turns. It is considered wide, with a main straight that is 60 feet across. The track has essentially no elevation change. There are wide runoff areas at most of the corners, which makes BIR's road course safe. The ground along the edge of the track is generally smooth except for some curbs, ditches, and low banks. The run-out areas have been re-graded within FIA compliance specifications. (BIR.)

The field moves to the back of the track in the 1981 Trans Am race. Turns 4 and 5 are the beginning of the S-curves that bring another dimension to the track. (JW.)

After moving through the mile-long front straight, drivers turn into the high-speed, right-hand, 60-degree Turn 1, which is intended to be taken flat out. Following Turn 1 is a straight that is sufficient to regain most or all of the speed scrubbed off in Turn 1. Turn 2 is a flat, high-speed, right-hand, 80-degree sweeper that can be taken flat out. Following Turn 2 is a long, generally flat runoff area and another straight long enough for drivers to regain much of the speed scrubbed off in Turn 2. The track dynamics allow for speed to be determined by aerodynamics and power rather than by torque and weight, as with slower tracks. Here, Cameron Lawrence's Chevy Camaro enters Turn 2. (JW.)

Turn 3 is a 130-degree, right-hand turn with a curb at the exit, followed by a short straight leading into the left-hand Turn 4. Turns 4, 5, and 6 are a set of S-curves with progressively longer straight stretches between them and curbs at the exits of all three. Turn 4 is a 100-degree, left-hand turn. Turns 5 and 6 are 90-degree right and left turns, both a little slower than Turn 4. The turns of the S-curves are far enough apart that drivers can get back across the track each time. Here, John Glowaski locks up a rear tire on his Dodge Neon coming into Turn 3 during the 2013 Jack Pine Sprints. (JW.)

Turn 7 is a higher-speed, 45-degree, left-hand turn that is followed very closely by Turn 8. Turn 7 requires a late apex, and drivers must stay to the left edge of the track to set up properly for Turn 8. The track surface is substantially widened at the entry to Turn 7 and again at the entry to Turn 8, which is a 75-degree, right-hand turn that is followed by a short straight leading into the fast 60-degree, right-hand Turn 9 under the vehicle access bridge. Here, Formula Vee's take Turn 9 coming under the bridge in 1979. (JW.)

The straight following Turn 9 is very long, and drivers can accelerate to make up lap time. The straight then moves into Turn 10, which is a fast and very wide 120-degree, right-hand turn leading out into the front straight. Drivers take Turn 10 as fast as they can because they are heading to the starter's stand to mark their track speed. New buildings erected at that turn over the last 20 years have only added to the excitement of a 120-degree turn taken at high speeds. Here, Stan Townes takes the checkered flag at the Formula Vee race at the 1979 Uncola Nationals. (JW.)

3

THE TRACK AGES

One of the ways any sports facility can make money is by offering suites. BIR built its Tower Suites facility in the late 1980s. The 11 suites overlook the drag-strip starting line and provide good sight lines for the drag strip. Each suite is air-conditioned and has a refrigerator, tables, chairs, couches, and a cable or live television feed from NHRA Nationals. Hot food and cold drinks are available for sale as well. (BIR.)

A three-story condominium complex was built in 2002 between the grandstand and the drag-strip staging area. Each condo has a kitchen, fireplace, two bathrooms, and two bedrooms. The units can be rented by the weekend throughout the season. (BIR.)

The NHRA took residence at BIR during the 1980s. BIR hosted the Winston Drag Racing Series, which is now part of the Lucas Oil NHRA Nationals, the track's biggest event each year.

The 3.1-mile road track was used sporadically for races, while the drag strip became the focal point of BIR's season. (BIR.)

While the driver gets the glory, the pit crew keeps the car running. Some drivers have professional pit crews, while others enlist friends or take care of the cars themselves. (BIR.)

Motorcycle racing also became very popular along the 3.1-mile road course, as well as on the drag strip. The Central Roadracing Association Superbike Series often races on the road course, while the drag racing course is used for other events. (BIR.)

In the 1990s and 2000s, rumors circulated that the track might be sold and converted into a resort, amusement park, or go-kart track. In 2006, Jed and Kristi Copham bought the track and brought their own vision to the future of the nearly 40-year-old facility. In addition to keeping the drag strip a main focus of business and a fan favorite, they wanted to separate the road course from the drag strip so that races could be run simultaneously. BIR is also home to the BIR Performance Driving School. (BIR.)

4

THE 2.5-MILE COMPETITION ROAD COURSE

When the Cophams bought BIR, it was home to several top NHRA drag races and CRA motorcycle races, but the number and quality of road races had diminished. In addition, the track had not kept up with changing safety rules. The Cophams chose to carve a shorter track through the infield that avoids the main straightaway. Now, BIR can run road and drag races simultaneously. Also, the 3.1-mile track remains intact, so when a road race is scheduled, the classic BIR track is available in the same configuration as when it opened in 1968. (BIR.)

The new 2.5-mile Competition Road Course combines Turns 1 through 7 from the Donnybrooke Road Course with a newly built track that runs through the infield. The new Turns 8 through 13 were added in 2008. The new course bypasses the straightaway, which allows it to continue to be used for drag racing. New owners Jed and Kristi Copham recognized that although BIR had been designed as a road track, drag racing had become both popular and profitable. By building the Competition Road Course with the drag strip in mind, they are able to offer quality road races while still maintaining a full schedule of drag races throughout the season. The Competition Road Course handles many kinds of races, including this 2013 CRA Superbike Race. (SDE Photography.)

Cliff Ebben's Ford Mustang uses the entire track as it comes out of Turn 12 during practice for the 2013 SCCA Trans Am Series race. Turns 4, 5, and 6 are a set of S-curves with progressively longer straight stretches between them. Turn 7 is a high-speed, left-hand, 45-degree turn. The new track deviates from the old at Turn 8, the Clover Leaf, which is a 300-degree corner that holds the car's threshold throughout the turn. Turn 9 is a gradual left leading to the left-hand Turn 10. Pit-in is off-line and to the left between Turns 10 and 11. Turn 11 is an increasing-radius corner right. A 1,000-foot straight leads to the 90-degree, left-hand Turn 12. Pit-out merges onto the track just after Turn 12. Turn 12 of the new 2.5- mile Competition Road Course is a nearly 90-degree turn that forces drivers to brake hard for Turn 12 before heading under the bridge and into a decreasing Turn 13 and then back onto the original track, merging with the original Turn 1. (JW.)

From Turn 12, a short 400-foot straight leads under the bridge to a decreasing-radius, right-hand Turn 13. It is about 1,400 feet back to Turn 1, where cars should still maintain a high rate of speed as they hit the banked corner. Here, Taylor Cuzick's Ford Fusion goes under the bridge and into Turn 13 during the 2013 Brainerd NASCAR K&N Series West race. The new road-race track has met with the approval of most drivers. (JW.)

Good-looking cars are good-looking cars no matter the course they are driven on. Tens of thousands of fans come to Brainerd's summer resort area each weekend to watch road races, drag races, and motorcycle races, and as a result the track's economic impact often brings more than $20 million to the area. (BIR.)

THE 2.5-MILE COMPETITION ROAD COURSE

5

A FANTASTIC FAN
EXPERIENCE

The fan experience has been the driving force behind the success of both Donnybrooke Speedway and Brainerd International Raceway. From rowdy camping all weekend in the Zoo at the far end of the course to genteel hot dog munching near the condominiums or grandstand, it is all about watching the cars and having fun. The following are some snapshots of the fans over the years. (BIR.)

There is never a shortage of fans for the Winston Cup Drag Racing Series, now called the Mello Yello Drag Racing Series, held every year at the track. "When I sat in the stands the first time and felt the rumbling of the cars, it was fantastic. I was hooked," said Cory Rustman, who has been attending the Lucas Oil NHRA National drag races at BIR every year since 1998, to the *Mankato Free Press* in 2013. (BIR.)

A FANTASTIC FAN EXPERIENCE

When the engines and stomachs stop rumbling, a different kind of drag racing emerges at the track. In its early years, fans were not permitted to stay on the grounds after races, causing much trouble in nearby towns. So campgrounds in the infield were added at BIR, including The Zoo, which is home to thousands of race fans during the Lucas Oil NHRA Nationals, many of whom came more for the social experience than to see the actual races. The top photograph is of the popular human rickshaw races in the Zoo, and below is a Radio Flyer one-man "Partywagon." (BIR.)

Fans get a glimpse of Paul Newman in 1980. (JW.)

In conjunction with the 1980 Uncola Nationals, there was a bed race held on the front quarter-mile drag strip. Each team consisted of four runners at each corner who rolled the bed down the course and one driver who directed the team. (Lew Winker.)

A FANTASTIC FAN EXPERIENCE

Some people have fun at the racetrack, and some people have a little too much fun at the racetrack. Race organizers are aware that a fan can see fast cars at any number of tracks, and being with friends and family on a nice summer day is what sells tickets. (BIR.)

Here are more examples of the engineering marvels that come to BIR as unique "Partywagons." They patrol the roads in The Zoo during the Lucas Oil NHRA Nationals. (BIR.)

A FANTASTIC FAN EXPERIENCE

Above, fans in the late 1960s take in a hot summer afternoon watching the races at BIR. Below, The 2012 "Partywagon" winners pose with Matt Hagen (left front), Jack Beckman (center front), and Ron Capps, all Pro Funny Car NHRA drivers. (BIR)

Longtime racer Warren Johnson, known as the "Professor of Pro Stock," also shared his thoughts on Brainerd: "Of course, no trip to Brainerd is complete without a tour of the campgrounds—that is an experience of its own. All in all, I'd say the fans make this race an event." (BIR.)

A FANTASTIC FAN EXPERIENCE

6

THROUGH
JERRY WINKER'S LENS

Growing up in the Twin Cities with a dual love for photography and racing, Jerry Winker used the first money he had ever saved to buy a Brownie Starlight camera. At age seven, he followed his father and brothers to Brainerd and started snapping photographs at the 1972 Donnybrooke Trans Am Series race. His father, Lew, took this photograph at that race. Since then, Jerry has never stopped. What follows is an amazing series of photographs taken by one man, at one place, since 1972—the photographs of Jerry Winker at BIR. (Lew Winker.)

With his first camera, Jerry took his first photograph: Bill Collins leading the Northwestern Bank Trans Am Series race at Donnybrooke with his AMC Javelin. (JW.)

George Follmer takes the winner's circle during that same race in 1972. (JW.)

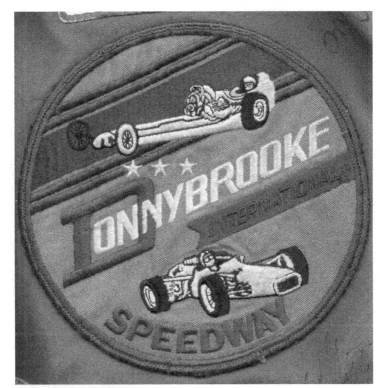

Jerry and his family have been going to both Donnybrooke and BIR since the track opened. Over the years, he has collected some snapshots of the track patches, the first of which is a rare look at the track's opening season (at right), one of only a few that remain in existence. The others are patches from the 1970s and early 1980s. (JW.)

Everyone wants to get a look at all of the hot cars, even the ones parked under a shady tree like Danny Ongais's Porsche 934 Turbo that ran in the 1976 Trans Am Series race. (JW.)

Prerace work goes well into the night to get Doug Peterson's Chevy Corvette ready for the second of two Trans Am rounds at BIR in 2012. (JW.)

Fans gather around Doug Rippie's Chevy Corvette 454 at the 1978 BIR Trans Am race after Rippie finished in eighth place. Greg Pickett and his Corvette 427 started in pole position and led for 22 laps before he got into an accident in the last lap and finished in fourth place. Jerry Hansen won the race in a DeKon Monza 1010. (JW.)

Ted Field (No. 0) and Danny Ongais (No. 00) and their Porsche 935 Turbos wait for the 1979 Pepsi Grand Prix to begin. It was a dominant year for that particular car, which was driven by four of the top five finishers: Peter Gregg, Ted Field, Charlie Mendez, and Ongais. David Hobbs was the odd man out in a BMW 320i. (JW.)

Above, Werner Frank's Porsche 934 gets offloaded for the 1979 Pepsi Grand Prix. Not only was the AMC Pacer an ugly car, it also did not race well either. Below, Robert Wood's Pacer is seen with a "For Sale" sign pasted in the back passenger window. (JW.)

John Cahill (above) takes out an Ocelot Sports 2000 at the 1980 Jack Pine Sprints, while Dan Olberg (below) races an Ocelot Mark 3. (JW.)

In addition to the Jack Pine Sprints, Jerry Winker captured Danny Sullivan and his Lola T5 30 at the 1980 Can-Am race (won by Patrick Tambay, also in a Lola). He also caught the start of the 1980 Trans Am Series race (won by Jon Bauer in a Porsche 911 SC). (JW.)

James Gaffney runs his classic RCA Formula Vee in the vintage races at BIR in 2013. (JW.)

Steve Beard, in the No. 53 Chevy Corvette, leads Bill Cammack, in the No. 88 Datsun 280Z, during the 1981 Trans Am Series race. Beard finished in 23rd place, while Cammack went out in Lap 16. (JW.)

Kathy Rude won a GTU-class victory at 24 Hours of Daytona in 1982 and had signed to make her debut in the 1984 Indy 500. Driving a Porsche 935 in the 1983 BIR Pepsi Grand Prix, however, she slammed into a stationary car while traveling at 180 miles per hour and suffered horrific injuries, ending her racing career. According to Jerry Winker, it was the worst wreck he has ever seen at BIR. (JW.)

Another female racer, Amy Ruman, drove her GT-1 Corvette to wins at BIR and New Jersey Motorsports Park in 2012. (JW.)

Small production cars take Turn 9 at the Jack Pine Sprints in 1981. (JW.)

John Paul Jr. (No. 18) passes John Fitzpatrick (No. 2) in the 1982 IMSA GT. Paul would win the race, placing ahead of Danny Ongais and Ted Field, both driving Lola T600s. Both Paul and Fitzpatrick were driving Porsche 935s. (JW.)

Michael Roe, seen above in a VDS-002, beat the pack in the 1983 Can-Am race. His fastest segment was Lap 23, which he took at an average of 124 miles per hour. Willie T. Ribbs (No. 3) drove his Mercury Capri to Trans Am wins in 1983, 1984, and 1985. His 1985 Capri is shown below. (JW.)

Hans Struck takes his Audi 200 Quattro for the win in the 1988 Trans Am Series race. That season, Quattros won in Dallas, Detroit, Niagara Falls, Cleveland, Brainerd, the Meadowlands, Mosport (Ontario), and St. Petersburg, but the car was outlawed by the end of the season for using four-wheel drive. (JW.)

Harvey West drives a Ford Mustang LX in the 1996 Jack Pine Sprints American Sedan runoffs. The Land O' Lakes chapter of the SCCA and BIR named their Memorial Day weekend races after West, who lived in Owatonna, Minnesota. (JW.)

Leighton Reese took his No. 6 Chevy Lumina in the 1989 American Stock Car Association race. (JW.)

Bobby (No. 30) and Tommy (No. 33) Archer were frequent winners with their Jeep Comanches at SCCA Racetruck Challenges. (JW.)

After a race day in 1999, SCCA members needed more action to satisfy them, so they set up an impromptu rallycross in the infield. Mark Utecht (above) drives a Volkswagen GTI rally car, while Katherine Freund (below) simply pulled her Dodge Neon from the parking lot to enter the race. (JW.)

Tony Ave (left) admires his trophy after winning the first of two Trans Am Series races at BIR in 2012. Cameron Lawrence's No. 11 Chevy Camaro, going into Turn 2 (below), is one of the top competitors in the SCCA Trans Am Series' newer TA2 category. (JW.)

Above, Group 1 cars line up on the false grid before the start of the 2012 Jack Pine Sprints Regionals. Below, Pat Goolsbey's Spec Racer Ford comes in on the hook later in the race. (JW.)

The Slugworks Racing Honda Civic has competed in all of the ChumpCar World Series at BIR since the series started here in 2010. The four-person team competes throughout the Midwest. (JW.)

THROUGH JERRY WINKER'S LENS

The ChumpCar World Series is a simple one: buy a car for $500, make the necessary safety modifications, and race. Not only is it fun, but it is also a great way to get some track time on a budget. Above, four BMWs, a Nissan, and a Ford battle for position while coming through Turn 4 at speed. Below, a wide variety of models head under the bridge at a ChumpCar race in 2013. (JW.)

Racing a car on ice is a time-honored tradition at BIR, as is pushing one back to the pits in sub-freezing temperatures as seen here with this Mazda RX7 rotary. (JW.)

Mark Utecht brings his Subaru Impreza around on the small lake at BIR. The track hosted ice racing in the past but has not had it on the schedule for several years. BIR has also hosted snocross and snowmobile endurance races in the past. (JW.)

The K&N Series West brings some real NASCAR action back to Brainerd. Michael Self leads Andrew Ranger during the closing laps of the 2013 race. Self went on to win the race for the second year in a row. (JW.)

Brian Kennedy's Shelby GT350 kicks up rocks at the inside of Turn 4 during the vintage race held in conjunction with the 2013 Trans Am race. (JW.)

Dave Schaal's Spec Racer Ford is seen entering Turn 13 at speed during the 2013 Jack Pine Sprints Regional races. (JW.)

Fire erupted inside one of the trailers during the 2013 Muscle Car Shootout. No one was injured—not even these two guys who were apparently unconcerned about flammable liquids in the area—but nothing could be salvaged. (JW.)

Sometimes the partying in the infield reaches new levels. This photograph was taken in 2013, but it could have been taken in any year since 1968. (JW.)

Mel Shaw's Chevy Camaro belches a huge flame coming through Turn 12 during the 2013 Trans Am race. (JW.)

The 2013 Trans Am race was one of the closest finishes in track history. In the end, the top four positions were separated by a scant 1.356 seconds. Doug Peterson was the winner of the event. (JW.)

Race winner Doug Peterson douses third-place finisher Amy Ruman with champagne after the 2013 Trans Am race. (JW.)

Jerry's brother, Mike, took these photographs at the 1979 Can-Am race. Above is Bobby Rahal's Prophet, and below is Jackie Ickx in his Lola T33 CS. Ickx won the race, beating Elliot Forbes-Robinson and his Spyder NF-11. Ickx came in with a time of 1:01:29.530, while Forbes-Robinson had a time of 1:01:57.850. Rahal placed third. (Mike Winker.)

THROUGH JERRY WINKER'S LENS

7

HOT RODS
AND FAST BIKES

The straightaway was meant for race cars to pit easily and to enter Turn 1 at top speed, but the nearly mile-long stretch has proven to be a fantastic drag race setup—a godsend for BIR during lean financial years. It was an easy sell, as all of the top racers, such as Doc Holliday and Don Prudhomme, and a top race, the Lucas Oil NHRA Nationals, have come to BIR. (BIR.)

The NHRA brought in Top Fuel and Funny Car Divisions to BIR in 1982 with the Champion Auto Stores Nationals and, later, the Lucas Oil NHA Nationals. With a 700-foot launchpad and more than 3,000 feet of shutdown—one of the longest on the NHRA tour—BIR is a favorite track to visit. For more than 30 years, the NHRA and the Lucas Oil NHRA Nationals have been an anchor for BIR. (JW.)

Drag racing has found a home at BIR's straightaway. At nearly one mile long, the concrete track provides copious room for a turnout. (Barry J. Bergeron, Eagle Eye Photography.)

Although the Lucas Oil NHRA Nationals is indeed a national race, BIR brings its own flavor to the event. A "pirate ship" can often be found in the camping ground (above), and snowmobile racing is an iconic fixture at the event, such as this one in 2013 (below). (Above, NHRA; below, NSA.)

HOT RODS AND FAST BIKES

The top racers in the country come to northern Minnesota for the Lucas Oil NHRA Nationals. The races feature some of the finest Top Fuel dragsters (above), Pro Stock (left), Funny Car, Pro Stock Motorcycle, and all other vehicle classes sponsored by NHRA. In 2005, Tony Schumacher clocked the fastest speed in the sport with a run of 337.58 miles per hour. Some of the others who compete at BIR include John Force, Ron Capps, and Kenny Bernstein. The Nationals also take place in late August, making the event one of the last chances for Minnesotans to get out, go camping, and enjoy the warm weather before school starts and the snow flies. (NHRA.)

Pro Stock Bike Racing—or motorcycle drag racing—has also been featured at BIR over the years. (Barry J. Bergeron, Eagle Eye Photography.)

The hard curves and fast straightaway that makes BIR a fantastic course for the Trans Am circuit also makes it a fantastic course for the Central Roadracing Association Superbike Series. (Barry J. Bergeron, Eagle Eye Photography.)

HOT RODS AND FAST BIKES

Racers come from all over the world to race at Nationals. (Barry J. Bergeron, Eagle Eye Photography.)

Die-hard fans will talk about the deafening sound as a dragster revs up for the green light and becoming hooked on the sheer power of the roar, but they also will tell you about how they enjoy the feeling of the ground quaking under their feet and the smell of the burning exhaust and rubber. Ray Fuchs (above) and his 1953 Studebaker race in the Pro Outlaw Class in the three-race Muscle Car Series. Larry Demers (below) and his 2006 Cobalt race in the Top Sportsman Class during the Thunder at the Lakes NHRA Divisional Race. (Barry J. Bergeron, Eagle Eye Photography.)

The American Motorcyclist Association ran its Superbike races at BIR for a number of years in the early 2000s. The racers in these photographs competed in one of four categories: Formula X, Supersport, Superstock, and Superbike. (Barry J. Bergeron, Eagle Eye Photography.)

The factors that made BIR a quality road-race track—good curves and a fantastic straightaway where riders can hit speeds well past 200 miles per hour—also worked in its favor as a motorcycle track. (Barry J. Bergeron, Eagle Eye Photography.)

8

WE'LL RACE ANYTHING

There is no shortage of vehicles with motors and wheels. BIR is a track for the masses, not the elite, and racing fans feel free to race anything into which they can put gas. BIR was a natural candidate to host the ISOC Amsoil Championship Snocross. In a snocross race, the track is groomed with several feet of snow, and some vertical challenges are added, giving a new look to the old track. (BIR.)

In 2004, the NSA brought its snowmobile-on-asphalt races to BIR. The idea is simple: take a stock snowmobile, make a few racing modifications (including a special track and skis with wheels), and see who can drag it the fastest. Above, Brian Bellman takes off in his adapted Ski-Doo. Below, Kristin Cartwright paces her modified Polaris against Bellman. (NSA.)

WE'LL RACE ANYTHING

Above, Kristin Cartwright blasts her modified sled against Brian Bellman. Below, Jamie Bellman brings his Polaris down the track. (NSA.)

Snowmobiles can also race on water. If revved at high speeds, they can skip like a stone without sinking. An accomplished rider can keep his machine going on an oval until he runs out of gas. The riders on this page, members of the International Watercross Association, come to BIR each year to race their sleds. Using the water in the middle of the infield, they race in a straight line and also around pylons. The IWA has had two races each year at BIR since 2012. (International Watercross Association.)

9

BIR PERFORMANCE
DRIVING SCHOOL

The BIR Performance Driving School owns a variety of cars ready for any level of racer with any level of experience. The experience is available for those who want to pilot a race car around the track or for those who simply want to bring their own cars to Brainerd and air them out for a while. (BIR.)

The school owns 17 Spec Racer Fords that, although able to hit 135 miles per hour on the track, are very safe. The school also offers ride-alongs in several exotics, including a Lotus, a Lamborghini, and a Corvette. An aerial shot of the track with the new road course superimposed over it shows how BIR is making the most use of the space available. (BIR.)

Using the new 2.5-mile track configuration helps drivers learn how to handle corners while keeping a steady speed and driving in traffic. (BIR.)

The school employs some of the best drivers in the country as instructors, such as Gary Curtis (above), who is the school's director and lead instructor, and Lon Weise (below). Many of the instructors have won on a variety of racing circuits. (BIR.)

DONNYBROOKE/BIR
RACE WINNERS

DATE	ORGANIZATION/RACE	WINNER
July 6, 1969	SCCA Trans Am	Parnelli Jones
September 13, 1969	USAC Stock Car	Don White
September 14, 1969	USAC Indy Car	Dan Gurney
September 14, 1969	USAC Indy Car	Gordon Johncock
July 5, 1970	SCCA Trans Am	Milt Minter
July 5, 1970	SCCA Trans Am U2	Horst Kwech
September 27, 1970	SCCA Can-Am	Denis Hulme
July 3, 1971	SCCA Two-Five Challenge	Bert Everett
July 4, 1971	SCCA Trans Am	Mark Donohue
September 12, 1971	SCCA Can-Am	Peter Revson
June 11, 1972	IMSA GT: 3 Hours of Brainerd	Denny Long
July 2, 1972	SCCA: Brown Photo Two-Five Challenge	Horst Kwech
July 4, 1972	SCCA Trans Am: Northwestern Banks	George Follmer
September 17, 1972	SCCA Can-Am	François Cevert
September 7, 1975	SCCA Trans Am	Jerry Hansen
August 15, 1976	SCCA Trans Am: 7UP Trans Am	Carl Shafer
June 19, 1977	IMSA GT: Pepsi Grand Prix	Danny Ongais
August 14, 1977	SCCA Trans Am: 7UP Trans Am	Peter Gregg
June 18, 1978	IMSA GT: Pepsi Grand Prix	Peter Gregg
August 13, 1978	SCCA Trans Am: Pepsi/7UP Trans Am	Jerry Hansen
June 17, 1979	IMSA GT: Pepsi Grand Prix	Peter Gregg
August 19, 1979	SCCA Can-Am	Jacky Ickx
June 15, 1980	IMSA GT: Pepsi Grand Prix	Luis Mendez
August 10, 1980	SCCA Trans Am	John Bauer
August 10, 1980	SCCA Formula Super Vee	Peter Kuhn
August 10, 1980	SCCA Can-Am	Patrick Tambay
June 14, 1981	IMSA GT: Pepsi Grand Prix	Klaus Ludwig
August 9, 1981	SCCA Trans Am	Bob Tullius
July 11, 1982	IMSA GT: Pepsi Grand Prix	John Paul Jr.
August 8, 1982	SCCA Trans Am	Paul Newman
July 10, 1983	IMSA GT: Pepsi Grand Prix	Al Holbert/ Jim Trueman
August 8, 1983	SCCA Trans Am: Pepsi Grand Prix	Willy T. Ribbs

July 22, 1984	SCCA Can-Am: Governor's Cup	Michael Roe
July 22, 1984	SCCA Trans Am: Pepsi Trans Am	Willy T. Ribbs
July 21, 1985	SCCA Trans Am	Willy T. Ribbs
July 20, 1986	SCCA Trans Am: Pepsi Grand Prix	Greg Pickett
July 19, 1987	SCCA Trans Am: Pepsi Grand Prix	Elliott Forbes-Robinson
July 17, 1988	SCCA Trans Am: Pepsi Grand Prix	Hans Joachim Stuck
July 23, 1989	SCCA Trans Am: Stroh's Light Grand Prix	Irv Hoerr
June 27, 1993	ASA Stock Car: Brainerd 300	Jimmy Spencer
June 26, 1994	ASA Stock Car: Pontiac Excitement 300	Butch Miller
June 25, 1995	ASA Stock Car: Pontiac Excitement 300	Scott Hansen
August 22, 2004	NASCAR Midwest Series: Cellular One 300	Brian Hoppe
September 5, 2010	SCCA Trans Am	Tony Ave
September 3, 2011	SCCA Trans Am	Tony Ave
September 4, 2011	SCCA Trans Am	Tony Ave
May 26, 2012	NASCAR West Series: Street Car Showdown	Michael Self
September 1, 2012	SCCA Trans Am: 25th Coca-Cola Muscle Car Shootout	Tony Ave
September 2, 2012	SCCA Trans Am:25th Coca-Cola Muscle Car Shootout	Amy Ruman
May 25, 2013	NASCAR West Series: NAPA Know How 125	Michael Self
September 1, 2013	SCCA Trans Am: 26th Muscle Car Shootout	Doug Peterson

Credit: UltimateRacingHistory.com

At BIR, every ticket includes a pit pass for all races, including the Lucas Oil NHRA Nationals. Fans can stand within several feet of where the race teams tear down the car and rebuild it between races. Drivers are accessible to the fans for autographs and questions. Here, Funny Car legend John Force signs autographs between runs during the 2012 Lucas Oil NHRA Nationals. (BIR.)

At BIR, every ticket includes a pit pass for all races, including the Lucas Oil NHRA Nationals. Fans can stand within several feet of where the race teams tear down the car and rebuild it between races. Drivers are accessible to the fans for autographs and questions. Here, Funny Car legend John Force signs autographs between runs during the 2012 Lucas Oil NHRA Nationals. (BIR.)

Visit us at
arcadiapublishing.com